The Official CHELSEA FC Annual 2013

Written by David Antill, Richard Godden, James Sugrue and Dominic Bliss

Designed by Jane Massey

A Grange Publication

© 2012. Published by Grange Communications Ltd., Edinburgh, under licence from Chelsea FC Merchandising Limited. www.chelseafc.com. Printed in the EU.

Photography © Getty Images, Press Association and Action Images

ISBN: 978-1-908925-03-9

£7.99

Hello Blue Geezers!

Welcome to the official Chelsea FC Annual 2013.

It has been a great year for Chelsea – we are UEFA Champions League winners and FA Cup winners and now we want to do even more for you, our fantastic supporters.

Inside you can find out about all of my team-mates – even the new ones – and about all the great moments we have enjoyed in 2012. You can also see the great history of this club – I'm so happy to be a Chelsea player and, like everyone who has ever worn the blue shirt, I play with pride for my team.

Keep supporting Chelsea and always stay positive.

Enjoy the life!

DAVID LUIZ

CONTENTS

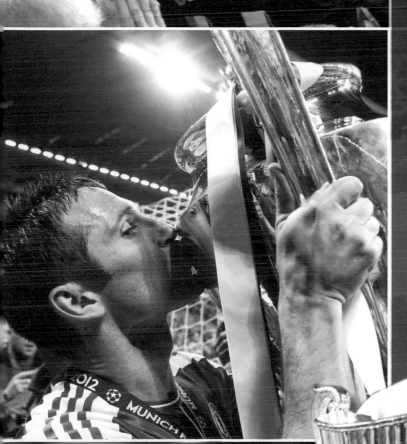

HONOURS LIST

LEAGUE TITLES: FOUR
1954/55, 2004/05,
2005/06, 2009/10

FA CUPS: SEVEN
1969/70, 1996/97,
1999/00, 2006/07,
2008/09, 2009/10, 2011/12

LEAGUE CUPS: FOUR
1964/65, 1997/98,
2004/05, 2006/07

UEFA CHAMPIONS LEAGUE: ONE
2011/12

EUROPEAN CUP WINNERS' CUP: TWO
1970/71, 1997/98

UEFA SUPER CUP: ONE
1998

COMMUNITY SHIELDS: FOUR
1955, 2000, 2005, 2009

FA YOUTH CUPS: FOUR
1959/60, 1960/61,
2009/10, 2011/12

LEAGUE WINNERS

STORY OF THE SEASON

The 2011/12 season will be forever remembered by Blues supporters as one of the greatest in the club's history. Here's how the boys made it an unforgettable campaign...

After winning three of our opening four Premier League games, the Blues made an equally impressive start in the UEFA Champions League. David Luiz showed his defensive skills to shut out Bayer Leverkusen and then went up the other end to score the opening goal in a 2-0 win!

Blues fans could get used to scoring five goals every week! This time Genk were on the receiving end, with Fernando Torres and Raul Meireles among the scorers in a 5-0 win – Chelsea's biggest-ever victory at Stamford Bridge in the UEFA Champions League.

Bolton Wanderers had no answer to Chelsea's attacking brilliance as Daniel Sturridge bagged two goals and Frank Lampard helped himself to a hat-trick in a 5-1 win. The only surprise was that we conceded a goal – Bolton hadn't scored against us at the Reebok Stadium since 2002!

November was a difficult month for the Blues, but Sturridge helped get December off to a perfect start as we beat Newcastle United 3-0. Lamps made his 500th start for Chelsea, but he missed the chance to mark the occasion with a goal when Tim Krul saved his penalty.

Chelsea had to beat Valencia to qualify from our UEFA Champions League group – and when the pressure is on, the Blues nearly always deliver! Didier Drogba scored twice and Ramires got the other in a brilliant 3-0 win which secured us a Round of 16 meeting with Italian side Napoli.

No one had beaten Man City in the Premier League in the 2011/12 season before they visited west London in December – but that's because they hadn't played Chelsea yet! Even though we went a goal down early on, Raul Meireles equalised and Lamps scored a penalty to win it for us.

Chelsea and Portsmouth met in the 2010 FA Cup Final and the two sides were drawn together in the third round this year. Although the Blues won 4-0, it took three late goals to make it safe, with energetic Brazilian midfielder Ramires scoring two of them.

Check out the tekkers from Juan Mata, whose superb penalty proved to be the difference between Chelsea and QPR in this west London derby.

You can always rely on Frank Lampard to get you a goal. This strike against Bolton Wanderers came in a 3-0 win and meant that Lamps became the first player to score at least ten Premier League goals in nine successive seasons. Not bad for a midfielder!

Roberto Di Matteo was all smiles after his first game as Chelsea's interim first-team coach. It came in the FA Cup – the competition in which he twice scored the winning goal in the Final as a player – as we beat Birmingham City to seal a quarter-final spot.

Gary Cahill scored his first goal for Chelsea in an entertaining 5-2 win over Leicester City. He marked the occasion with a message for his former Bolton Wanderers team-mate Fabrice Muamba, who was seriously ill at the time.
Gaz is not just a great footballer, he's a lovely guy!

After losing the first leg to Napoli 3-1, the Blues looked to be heading out of the UEFA Champions League. However, a stunning fightback saw us win 4-1 in the second leg – and the winning goal came from defender Branislav Ivanovic in extra time!

He may have only scored five goals for the Blues in 2011/12, but Salomon Kalou didn't net a more important one than his winner against Benfica in the UEFA Champions League quarter-final. And what an assist by Fernando Torres – that's what we call team work!

The Blues were hanging on to our lead against Benfica in the second leg when Raul Meireles scored an absolute worldie to make the game safe. And, after their supporters had given him plenty of stick for being a former Porto player, the midfielder certainly enjoyed the moment!

TOTTENHAM HOTSPUR **1**
BALE 56'

CHELSEA **5**
DROGBA 43', MATA 49'
RAMIRES 77', LAMPARD 81'
MALOUDA 90'

CHELSEA SUBSTITUTIONS: CAHILL ON FOR

It's a sight no Chelsea fan will ever get tired of: a scoreboard that reads Tottenham Hotspur 1-5 Chelsea. Spurs may have finished ahead of us in the Premier League, but they had no answer for our attacking brilliance in the FA Cup semi-final.

The UEFA Champions League paired us with Barcelona yet again and Didier Drogba just loves playing against the Spanish clubs. Reputations don't matter to Didier. He needed just one chance to secure a crucial 1-0 win to take into the second leg...

"He scores when he wants!" Fernando Torres took the confidence of his goal in the Nou Camp into our game against QPR, when he scored a hat-trick as we thrashed our neighbours 6-1!

One of the greatest comebacks ever! 2-0 down on the night, down to 10 men and playing against one of the best sides in Europe, but strikes from Ramires – which won Goal of the Season, no less – and a brilliant last-minute effort by Fernando Torres put us through to our second UEFA Champions League Final. What a night!

Ramires and Didier Drogba may have taken the headlines for scoring the goals in our 2-1 FA Cup Final win over Liverpool, but let's not forget this wonder-save from Petr Cech. The Blues No 1 showed why he is one of the best in the world – and why all Chelsea supporters love him!

Chelsea looked to be crashing to defeat in the UEFA Champions League Final until Didier Drogba scored this incredible header against Bayern Munich. And when the final penalty was to be taken in the shoot-out, who was there to take it? You guessed it – that man Drogba!

FA CUP HISTORY

CHELSEA FOOTBALL CLUB

1970   1997   2000   2007   2009   2010   2012

CHELSEA FOOTBALL CLUB

Chelsea became the joint-fourth most successful club in FA Cup history when we beat Liverpool in the Final last season – here's how we won the world's oldest club competition prior to that.

1

Ron Chopper Harris and Peter Osgood
2 – 1 win over Leeds United 1970

2

1997 Roberto Di Matteo scored a goal in
the first 43 seconds of the Final

3

Di Matteo the scorer and skipper Dennis Wise held aloft the FA Cup in 2000.

Captain Ron "Chopper" Harris and Peter Osgood, who scored in every round, celebrate the club's first FA Cup triumph in 1970 following a 2-1 win over Leeds United in the Final after the first game had finished 1-1.

 It was a long wait for Chelsea fans, but the Blues lifted the trophy for a second time in 1997 after a 2-0 win over Middlesbrough, aided by Roberto Di Matteo's goal after just 43 seconds in the Final.

 The last-ever Final at the old Wembley Stadium saw the Blues record a 1-0 victory over Aston Villa. Di Matteo was the scorer once again and skipper Dennis Wise held aloft the FA Cup with son Henry.

 Wembley Stadium re-opened in 2007 and the first FA Cup Final at the new ground saw Chelsea take on Manchester United, with Didier Drogba scoring the game's only goal in extra-time to hand the Blues a fourth triumph in the competition.

 Chelsea had to recover from the shock of conceding the fastest goal in an FA Cup Final to defeat Everton. Louis Saha netted for the Toffees after 25 seconds, but Drogba and Frank Lampard had the last laugh.

 Wembley goal machine Drogba continued his remarkable record at the stadium, scoring a sublime free-kick against Portsmouth to give Chelsea a 1-0 victory. That handed the Blues an historic "Double" as we also won the Premier League title.

Goalkeepers

1 PETR CECH
Born Plzen, Czech Republic, 20.5.82
Height 1.96m (6ft 5in)
Signed from Rennes (July 2004)
Chelsea debut Man Utd (h) 15.8.04. Won 1-0
Appearances 368+1 **Clean sheets** 178

Did You Know? *Petr has been named Czech Republic Player of the Season a record seven times.*

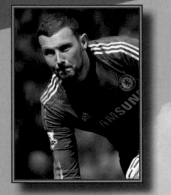

22 ROSS TURNBULL
Born Bishop Auckland, 4.1.85
Height 1.93m (6ft 4in)
Signed from Middlesbrough (July 2009)
Chelsea debut Bolton (h) League Cup 28.10.09, substitute for Hilario. Won 4-0
Appearances 10+2 **Clean sheets** 0+2

Did You Know? *When Chelsea beat Fulham in the Carling Cup in 2011, Ross kept out a penalty in normal time and two in the penalty shoot-out.*

40 HENRIQUE HILARIO
Born São Pedro da Cova, Portugal, 21.10.75
Height 1.89m (6ft 2in)
Signed from CD Nacional (May 2006)
Chelsea debut Barcelona (h) UEFA Champions League 18.10.06.
Won 1-0 **Appearances** 35+4 **Clean sheets** 16+2

Did You Know? *Hilario made his debut for the Portuguese national team at the age of 34 in a 2-0 win against China.*

Defenders

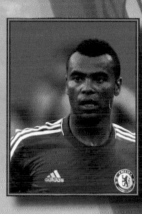

2 BRANISLAV IVANOVIC

Born Sremska Mitrovica, Serbia, 22.2.84
Height 1.85m (6ft 1in)
Signed from Lokomotiv Moscow (January 2008)
Chelsea debut Portsmouth (a) League Cup 24.9.08. Won 4-0

Appearances 146+14 **Goals** 14

Did You Know? *Branislav earned the nickname "Two Goal"
after he netted his first two goals for the club in a 3-1 win over
Liverpool in the 2008/09 UEFA Champions League quarter-final.*

3 ASHLEY COLE

Born Stepney, 20.12.80
Height 1.76m (5ft 9in)
Signed from Arsenal (August 2006)
Chelsea debut Charlton (h) 9.9.06, substitute for Wayne Bridge. Won 2-1

Appearances 251+10 **Goals** 6

Did You Know? *Ash is England's most-capped left-back
after overtaking Kenny Sansom's tally of 86 in February 2011.*

4 DAVID LUIZ

Born Diadema, Brazil, 22.4.87
Height 1.89m (6ft 2in)
Signed from Benfica (January 2011)
Chelsea debut Liverpool (h) 6.2.11, substitute for José Bosingwa. Lost 0-1

Appearances 48+4 **Goals** 5

Did You Know? *David Luiz scored in both of his first two Premier
League games against Manchester United at Stamford Bridge*

19 PAULO FERREIRA

Born Cascais, Portugal, 18.1.79
Height 1.83m (6ft)
Signed from Porto (July 2004)
Chelsea debut Man Utd (h) 15.8.04.

Did You Know? *Ferreira played his 200th match for
Chelsea in a 3–1 win over Birmingham on the
20th April 2011.*

1st team SQUAD PROFILES

Defenders

24 GARY CAHILL
Born Sheffield, 19.12.85
Height 1.88m (6ft 2in)
Signed from Bolton Wanderers (January 2012)
Chelsea debut Man Utd (h) 5.2.12. Drew 3-3
Appearances 16+3 **Goals** 2

Did You Know? *Gary appeared in the first-ever match at the new Wembley Stadium in 2007 when England Under-21s drew 3-3 with Italy.*

26 JOHN TERRY
Born Barking, 7.12.80
Height 1.87m (6ft 2in)
Turned pro March 1998
Chelsea debut Aston Villa (h) League Cup 28.10.98, substitute for Dan Petrescu. Won 4-1
Appearances 526+21 **Goals** 49

Did You Know? *JT has been named as UEFA's most valuable defender on three occasions.*

28 CESAR AZPILICUETA
Born Pamplona, Spain 28.8.89
Height 1.78m (5ft 10in)
Signed from Marseille (August 2012)

Did You Know? *Cesar was signed for his former club Marseille by Didier Deschamps, who played for Chelsea in the 1999/00 season*

34 RYAN BERTRAND
Born Southwark, 5.8.89
Height 1.79m (5ft 10in)
Signed from Gillingham (July 2005)
Chelsea debut Birmingham (h) 20.4.11, substitute for Ashley Cole. Won 3-1
Appearances 13+3 **Goals** 0

Did You Know? *Ryan played 161 games at lower-league level before making his first-team debut for the Blues.*

Midfielders

6 ORIOL ROMEU

Born Ulldecona, Spain, 24.9.91
Height 1.83m (6ft 0in)
Signed from Barcelona (August 2011)
Chelsea debut Sunderland (a) 10.9.11, substitute for Nicolas Anelka. Won 2-1
Appearances 17+7 **Goals** 0

Did You Know? *Romeu made his official debut for Chelsea on 10 September 2011, being brought on as a substitute in the 79th minute of the 2-1 away win against Sunderland.'*

7 RAMIRES

Born Barra do Pirai, Brazil, 24.3.87
Height 1.78m (5ft 10in)
Signed from Benfica (August 2010)
Chelsea debut Stoke (h) 28.8.10, substitute for Michael Essien. Won 2-0
Appearances 77+11 **Goals** 14

Did You Know? *Ramires became the first Brazilian to score in an FA Cup Final when he opened the scoring in the Blues' 2-1 victory over Liverpool last season.*

8 FRANK LAMPARD

Born Romford, 20.6.78
Height 1.84m (6ft)
Signed from West Ham (June 2001)
Chelsea debut Newcastle (h) 19.8.01. Drew 1-1
Appearances 522+36 **Goals** 186

Did You Know? *At the start of the 2012/13 season Frank will require just 17 more goals to become Chelsea's all-time leading goalscorer, overtaking Bobby Tambling, who played for the club in the Sixties and Seventies*

10 JUAN MATA

Born Burgos, Spain, 28.4.88
Height 1.70m (5ft 7in)
Signed from Valencia (August 2011)
Chelsea debut Norwich (h) 27.8.11. Won 3-1, substitute for Florent Malouda, scored the final goal. **Appearances** 47+7 **Goals** 12

Did You Know? *Juan became the first man to win Chelsea's Player of the Year award in his debut campaign at the club since Ruud Gullit in 1995/96.*

Midfielders

11 OSCAR

Born Americana, Brazil, 9.9.91
Height 1.79m (5ft 10in) Signed from Internacional (July 2012)

Did You Know? *Oscar scored a hat-trick in the 2011 Under-20 World Cup Final as Brazil beat Portugal 3-2 to lift the trophy.*

12 JOHN MIKEL OBI

Born Jos, Nigeria, 22.4.87
Height 1.88m (6ft 2in)
Signed from Lyn Oslo (July 2006)
Chelsea debut Liverpool (Millennium Stadium) FA Community Shield 13.8.06, substitute for Paulo Ferreira. Lost 1-2
Appearances 192+47 **Goals** 2

Did You Know? *Both of John's goals for Chelsea came in the FA Cup in his first season with the club – and the Blues went on to lift the trophy by beating Manchester United in the Final.*

13 VICTOR MOSES

Born Kaduna, Nigeria 12.12.90
Height 1.77m (5ft 10in)
Signed from Wigan Athletic (August 2012)
Did You Know? *Victor attended the Whitgift School in Croydon, where he received football coaching from former Chelsea captain Colin Pates!*

15 FLORENT MALOUDA

Born Cayenne, French Guiana, 13.6.80
Height 1.77m (5ft 10in)
Signed from Lyon (July 2007)
Chelsea debut Man Utd (Wembley) FA Community Shield 5.8.07.

Lost 0-3 on penalties after a 1-1 draw in normal time. Scored the equalising goal.
Appearances 173+56 **Goals** 45

Did You Know? *Flo was Chelsea's highest scorer in the Premier League in the 2010/11 season, netting 13 goals.*

Midfielders

21 MARKO MARIN
Born Bosanska Gradiska, Yugoslavia 13.3.89
Height 1.70m (5ft 7in)
Signed from Werder Bremen (July 2012)

Did You Know? *Marin was already popular with Chelsea fans before his arrival as he once scored for Werder Bremen in a UEFA Champions League game against Spurs!*

Forwards

9 FERNANDO TORRES
Born Madrid, Spain, 20.3.84
Height 1.86m (6ft 1in)
Signed from Liverpool (January 2011)
Chelsea debut Liverpool (h) 6.2.11. Lost 0-1
Appearances 43+24 **Goals** 12

Did You Know? *Fernando scored the winning goal for Spain in the final of the 2008 European Championship against Germany.*

17 EDEN HAZARD
Born La Louviere, Belgium, 7.1.91
Height 1.72m (5ft 8in) Signed from Lille (July 2012)

Did You Know? *Before signing for Chelsea, Eden was named Player of the Year for the past two seasons in France. And in each of the previous two seasons he was named Young Player of the Year!*

23 DANIEL STURRIDGE
Born Birmingham, 1.9.89
Height 1.88m (6ft 2in)
Signed from Manchester City (July 2009). Chelsea debut Sunderland (a) 18.8.09, substitute for Didier Drogba. Won 3-1
Appearances 47+37 **Goals** 22

Did You Know? *Daniel was Chelsea's joint-leading scorer in the 2011/12 Premier League season, finishing tied with Frank Lampard on 11.*

THE GAFFER

Having enjoyed cup success as a Blues player, Roberto Di Matteo proved to have the same knack in his spell as interim first-team coach, leading us to glory in both the FA Cup and UEFA Champions League. That led to a permanent appointment during the summer and the former Italian international expressed his desire to help the club move forward after the triumphs of 2011/12.

Di Matteo took charge of team affairs for the first time for an FA Cup fifth-round replay victory over Birmingham City at the start of March. Less than two months later, the Blues were lifting the trophy following a 2-1 win against Liverpool at Wembley.

It certainly wasn't the first time the former Blues midfielder had made a big impact on the competition. One of his defining moments as a Chelsea player came in the 1997 Final when he found the back of the net with a scorching 30-yarder after just 43 seconds to set us on the road to a 2-0 win over Middlesbrough and our first major piece of silverware since 1971. It was the fastest FA Cup Final goal of all time until Louis Saha broke the record, against Chelsea, in 2009.

As well as scoring in the 1998 League Cup Final – another 2-0 win over Middlesbrough – Di Matteo grabbed another Wembley goal – this time in our 1-0 win against Aston Villa in 2000 in the last-ever FA Cup Final before the old stadium was demolished. At the time Robbie said: "It's a shame they're tearing the old place down – it has been a very lucky ground for me." Little did he know that 12 years later he would be masterminding another triumph for the Blues in the new national stadium!

Did you know?
Di Matteo is the fourth Italian to manage Chelsea, following in the footsteps of Gianluca Vialli, Claudio Ranieri and Carlo Ancelotti.

Roberto Di Matteo factfile

Date of birth: 29 May 1970
Place of birth: Schaffhausen, Switzerland

Playing career

Previous clubs:
Schaffhausen, Zurich, Aarau, Lazio

Chelsea stats:
175 apps, 26 goals

Chelsea honours:
2 FA Cups (1997 & 2000), 1998 European Cup Winner's Cup; 1998 League Cup

International appearances:
34 Italian caps, 2 goals

Managerial career

Previous clubs: Milton Keynes Dons, West Bromwich Albion

Chelsea stats (at end of 2011/12 season): 21 games, won 13, drawn 5, lost 3

Meet some of the new boys

Belgian forward Eden Hazard, German midfielder Marko Marin and Oscar were the first three signings of an exciting summer for the Blues.

Eden Hazard

Regarded as one of Europe's most exciting young talents, the Blues beat off competition from a number of other clubs to snap up Hazard. Despite being just 21 years old, the skilful forward has already won 28 caps for the Belgium national side and accumulated an impressive array of honours with former club Lille, where he played alongside former Chelsea star Joe Cole last season.

Factfile
DOB: 7/1/1991
Position: Forward
Honours: 2010/11 Ligue 1 title,
2010/11 Coupe de France,
Ligue 1 Player of the Year 2009 & 2010,
Ligue 1 Young Player of the Year 2009 & 2010,
Ligue 1 Team of the Year 2010, 2011 & 2012

Did You Know?
Eden comes from a footballing family. His dad played in the Belgian Second Division, his mum also played the game and his brother Thorgan was recently signed to Chelsea Under-21s. He has two other brothers who also show signs of promise.

Marko Marin

The Blues agreed a deal to sign Marin from German side Werder Bremen in April and he linked up with his new team-mates for pre-season training at the start of July. The 23-year-old has earned 16 caps for Germany and is known for his acceleration, dribbling and creativity.
He can play as a winger or in the centre of midfield.

Factfile
DOB: 13/3/1989
Position: Midfielder
Honours: 2007/08 Bundesliga 2
2009 UEFA European Under-21 Football winners medal
2010 FIFA World Cup Bronze medal

Did You Know?
Marko made two substitute appearances at the 2010 World Cup. He came on in the 4-0 win over Australia and in a 1-0 defeat to Serbia, helping the Germans finish third in the tournament.

Oscar

Chelsea's third signing of the summer saw the addition of another hugely talented youngster in the shape of Brazilian international Oscar.
The attacking midfielder previously played for Internacional in his homeland and had attracted the attentions of top clubs around the world.
He possesses awesome acceleration with and without the ball, sensational dribbling skills and a powerful shot, meaning he is sure to be a big hit with Blues fans.

Factfile
DOB: 9/9/1991
Position: Midfielder

Honours: FIFA Under-20 World Cup

Did You Know?
Oscar is the seventh Brazilian to play for Chelsea, following in the footsteps of Emerson Thome, Alex, Juliano Belletti, Mineiro, Ramires and David Luiz.

Eden Hazard

Marko Marin

Oscar

Farewell Drogba

2012 was the year Chelsea said goodbye to Didier Drogba, our UEFA Champions League Final goal-scoring hero and a true Stamford Bridge legend.

Having arrived from Marseille in 2004, he spent eight years at Chelsea, making 341 appearances and scoring an incredible 157 goals. In fact, that goals tally makes him the fourth-highest goal-scorer in the history of the club, behind only Bobby Tambling, Kerry Dixon and Frank Lampard.

In his time leading the line for the Blues, Drogba lifted the Premier League trophy three times, the FA Cup four times, the Carling Cup twice and, finally, the UEFA Champions League. In other words, he won the lot!

Drogba was, quite simply, a winner. His record when playing in finals for Chelsea was outstanding – nine goals in nine finals! He confirmed that reputation with crucial goals in both the FA Cup and UEFA Champions League Finals in his final month as a Chelsea player.

Farewell Didier

You will always be a hero at the Bridge!

Didier Drogba season by season

2004/05 season
Premier League:	18+8 apps;	10 goals
UEFA Champions League:	8+1 apps;	5 goals
FA Cup:	1+1 apps;	0 goals
Carling Cup:	3+1 apps;	1 goal
Total:	**30+11 apps;**	**16 goals**

2005/06 season
Premier League:	20+9 apps;	12 goals
UEFA Champions League:	5+2 apps;	1 goal
FA Cup:	3 apps;	1 goal
Carling Cup:	0+1 apps;	0 goals
Community Shield:	1 app;	2 goals
Total:	**29+12 apps;**	**16 goals**

2006/07 season
Premier League:	32+4 apps;	20 goals
UEFA Champions League:	12 apps;	6 goals
FA Cup:	6 apps;	3 goals
Carling Cup:	3+2 apps;	4 goals
Community Shield:	1 app;	0 goals
Total:	**54+6 apps;**	**33 goals**

2007/08 season
Premier League:	17+2 apps;	8 goals
UEFA Champions League:	11 apps;	6 goals
FA Cup:	0+1 apps;	0 goals
Carling Cup:	1 app;	1 goal
Total:	**29+3 apps;**	**15 goals**

2008/09 season
Premier League:	15+9 apps;	5 goals
UEFA Champions League:	7+3 apps;	5 goals
FA Cup:	5+1 apps;	3 goals
Carling Cup:	2 apps;	1 goal
Total:	**29+13;**	**14 goals**

2009/10 season
Premier League:	31+1 apps;	29 goals
UEFA Champions League:	5 apps;	3 goals
FA Cup:	4 apps;	3 goals
Carling Cup:	0+2 apps;	2 goals
Community Shield:	1 app;	0 goals
Total:	**41+3 apps;**	**37 goals**

2010/11 season
Premier League:	30+6 apps;	11 goals
UEFA Champions League:	5+2 apps;	2 goals
FA Cup:	2 apps;	0 goals
Carling Cup:	0 apps;	0 goals
Community Shield:	0+1 apps;	0 goal
Total:	**37+9 apps;**	**13 goalS**

2011/12 season
Premier League:	16+8 apps;	5 goals
UEFA Champions League:	7+1 apps;	6 goals
FA Cup:	2+1 apps;	2 goals
Carling Cup:	0 apps;	0 goals
Total:	25+10 apps;	13 goals
Overall Total:	**274+67 apps;**	**157 goals**

CHELSEA HISTORY
1997

FA Cup Winners Again!
Wembley 1997

Younger supporters of Chelsea may have become used to seeing their club lift silverware on a regular basis, but it certainly wasn't always like that.

Back in 1997, it had been 26 years since any major cups had found their way into the Stamford Bridge trophy cabinet, but there was a feeling that this would be the year for things to change.

Led by Dutch legend Ruud Gullit, the Blues boasted players of international repute among their number for the first time in many years and they travelled to Wembley for the FA Cup Final in May to face a Middlesbrough side that had just been relegated from the Premier League.

Within 43 seconds of the start of the Final, Chelsea went ahead! Roberto Di Matteo, in his first season in England, pushed the ball inside the opposition half and let fly with a thunderbolt from his right boot that flew past Ben Roberts, the Middlesbrough goalkeeper, and hit the bottom of the crossbar before bouncing down over the line. It was the perfect start to the game and Di Matteo ran roaring towards the Chelsea fans in the spring sunshine, with his fists clenched in celebration.

The game was settled by another Chelsea central-midfielder seven minutes from the end. This time it was defensive midfield man, Eddie Newton, who got his name on the score sheet and confirmed that the Blues supporters, who had waited so long for success, would get to celebrate that day.

Dan Petrescu's cross from the right looked to be going out for a goal kick, but Gianfranco Zola – the Footballer of the Year for 1997 – leaped to flick the ball back into the danger area with his heel and there was Newton to force the ball home.

It was a game that will surely never be forgotten by the Blues who were there. There was a feeling that it would be the start of something special and the team's official song for the Final – "Blue Day" by Suggs and Co – included the line: "Will there ever be a Blue tomorrow?" before captain Dennis Wise offered the response: "Believe it, all right!"

The skipper was right. Chelsea have never looked back since lifting the famous old trophy that day in 1997. The following year saw Gianluca Vialli take over as manager from Gullit mid-season and the Italian steered the team to the League Cup and European Cup Winners' Cup, as well as the UEFA Super Cup.

It laid the foundations for a period of Chelsea success that has moved onto a new level since Roman Abramovic bought the club in 2003. The rest is history, but 1997 will always remain one of the greatest of all the "Blue Days" this club has enjoyed.

Did you know?

Chelsea went on to beat Middlesbrough at Wembley once again a year later, winning 2-0 after extra time in the League Cup Final in 1998. Roberto Di Matteo, the man for the big occasion, was one of the goal heroes that day as well!

Match Facts:

Chelsea 2 Middlesbrough 0

Scorers:	Roberto Di Matteo, Eddie Newton
Venue:	Wembley
Attendance:	79,160
Date:	17 May 1997

Farewell to Help A Capital Child

Chelsea said goodbye to Help a Capital Child in the summer after three fantastic seasons as our national charity partner.

The official charity of radio station Capital FM thanked the club at the last home game of the 2011/12 season against Blackburn Rovers

Since the partnership began they have raised £621,621.22 with the Blues for their work with young people in London and around the UK.

Capital FM presenter and Help a Capital Child ambassador Lisa Snowdon said: "I've visited many of the projects that Help a Capital Child have funded thanks to the support of Chelsea FC, and seen for myself the massive impact it has on the lives of so many kids."

Snowdon launched the partnership in 2009 at Chelsea's training ground with help from fellow radio presenter Johnny Vaughan, local children and the Blues players. They even got to join in a penalty competition with Frank Lampard and Petr Cech. Last season, Chelsea's Premier League home game against Everton was dedicated to Help a Capital Child's Teenage Cancer Trust appeal.

There was also a day of fund-raising at Stamford Bridge in December based around an open training session at the stadium, plus Chelsea Foundation coaches and Stamford the Lion entertaining fans off the pitch.

Help a Capital Child even auctioned the chance to be a Chelsea mascot for the day. The three lucky winners all got to walk out onto the pitch at the Bridge with captain John Terry, before our match with Queens Park Rangers.

RIGHT TO PLAY

For the eighth season Chelsea players will put smiles on children's faces around the world by working with global charity partner Right To Play.

The Charity helps 800,000 children each week in over 20 countries by giving them the chance to play games and sports. That is something most of us take for granted, but in places suffering from conflict, poverty or disease it can make a huge difference to their lives and help teach important lessons.

The Chelsea players wore the Right To Play logo on the backs of their shirts as they won last season's UEFA Champions League. The first time was in the 1-1 draw at Genk and the charity thanked the Blues by giving Chairman Bruce Buck and Chief Executive Ron Gourlay a certificate at our next home game in the competition. It remained on the Chelsea shirts for every European game, including the final against Bayern Munich.

Right To Play have also been part of the last two pre season tours, in Asia and America. The team showed their support on both continents by each player carrying a Red Ball with Right To Play's motto "Look after yourself, look after one another" written on it. The players then kicked the special balls into the crowd for the fans.

In England, the Right To Play World Cup Challenge has been held at Stamford Bridge for the last six years. The football tournament raised over £120,000 for the charity in 2012 as teams competed for the trophy under the names of countries where Right To Play helps children.

CHELSEA Foundation

The Chelsea Foundation was started in 2010 and looks after all the club's community work and charity fund-raising.

Over the last two years it has gone from strength to strength, both in its own projects and working with other charities at home in the UK and around the world.

The Foundation aims to use the power and popularity of football, and especially Chelsea, to support a wide range of good causes from education to the environment, with the players themselves playing a big part.

Education Through Football is one of the main projects helping young people succeed at school. Last season midfielder Oriol Romeu visited Servite Roman Catholic Primary School in London for a Kickstart Spanish lesson, handing out certificates and speaking to pupils in the language of his home, Spain.

Children from lots of London schools also get Kickstart Maths lessons at Stamford Bridge and famous author and artist Michael Foreman gave a special lesson at Chelsea's training ground on drawing and story-writing as part of the Education Through Football project.

The first-team squad take time out every Christmas to visit Chelsea & Westminster Hospital, so they can cheer up people who are too ill to enjoy the holiday at home.

The Foundation also promotes disability football both by arranging their own teams and introducing people to the sport.

The charity even works to level the playing field for the under-represented Asian communities when it comes to starting a career in professional football. The annual Asian Star event invites young players from Asian backgrounds to impress the Chelsea coaches at Cobham, with this year's best getting a year-long place at an Elite Training Centre.

As well as charity work, the Chelsea Foundation holds Soccer Schools during the holidays for those who want to learn to play football like the Blues. Captain John Terry even handed out the trophies at one summer residential camp in 2011.

Children from lots of London schools also get Kickstart Maths lessons at Stamford Bridge and famous author and artist Michael Foreman gave a special lesson at Chelsea's training ground on drawing and story-writing as part of the Education Through Football project.

Education Through Football is one of the main projects helping young people succeed at school. Last season midfielder Oriol Romeu visited Servite Roman Catholic Primary School in London for a Kickstart Spanish lesson, handing out certificates and speaking to pupils in the language of his home, Spain.

The charity even works to level the playing field for the under-represented Asian communities when it comes to starting a career in professional football. The annual Asian Star event invites young players from Asian backgrounds to impress the Chelsea coaches at Cobham, with this year's best getting a year-long place at an Elite Training Centre.

Graeme Le Saux and Olympic gold medal sprinter Darren Campbell taking part in a Chelsea Foundation and Premier League 4 Sport event at the St Mary Magdalene Academy school in Islington, London

As well as charity work, the Chelsea Foundation holds Soccer Schools during the holidays for those who want to learn to play football like the Blues. Captain John Terry even handed out the trophies at one summer residential camp in 2011.

Chelsea Foundation
LOTTERY
SUPPORTING OUR COMMUNITIES

Date 20 November 2011

Pay **Aroha Tam**

One Thousand Nine Hundred

& Five Pounds

£1,905

SUPPORTING OUR COMMUNI

The first-team squad take time out every Christmas to visit Chelsea & Westminster Hospital, so they can cheer up people who are too ill to enjoy the holiday at home.

SPAIN

Fernando Torres and Juan Mata helped Spain make history at Euro 2012. Not only did they both score in the record biggest final win of all time – 4-0 against Italy – but they also became the first team ever to lift the trophy at a World Cup and two European Championships in a row.

Torres will be especially happy after becoming the first player to score in two Euro finals, before setting up Chelsea team-mate Mata for Spain's fourth. That also meant Torres came away from the tournament with the Golden Boot thanks to his three goals and one assist.

Both players now join an elite group from football history to have won the UEFA Champions League and European Championship in the same year, which only five people had done before.

PORTUGAL

Raul Meireles fell one game short of the final after coming up against fellow Blues Torres and Mata's Spain in the semis. The Portuguese still went home from Poland and Ukraine with their heads held high, though, after making their way through the "Group of Death" with wins over Denmark and Holland, before seeing off the Czech Republic in the last eight with a hard-fought 1-0 victory.

FRANCE

Florent Malouda also had his dream of lifting the trophy ended by Torres and Mata in the quarter-finals. That 2-0 loss wasn't the first time he'd faced some familiar opponents though, after taking on England in France's opening group game, a 1-1 draw.

ENGLAND

An England squad without the injured Chelsea duo Frank Lampard and Gary Cahill gave everything at Euro 2012, but even the defensive skill of John Terry and Ashley Cole couldn't take them past the quarter-finals, where they lost on penalties to Italy. Cole will definitely remember the last group game against former Blues striker Andriy Shevchenko's Ukraine, when the left-back broke the record for playing the most games for England at a tournament.

CZECH REPUBLIC

Petr Cech was the first Chelsea player to make it into the knockout rounds when the Czech Republic finished top of Group A. The goalkeeper repeated some of the heroics that helped the Blues to UEFA Champions League glory and took the captain's armband for their last two games, but Raul Meireles and Portugal ended his tournament in the quarter-finals.

EURO 2000

Torres and Mata aren't the first pair from Chelsea to lift the European Championship trophy. At Euro 2000, Marcel Desailly and Didier Deschamps lined up for France and won the final against Italy in extra time with a Golden Goal.

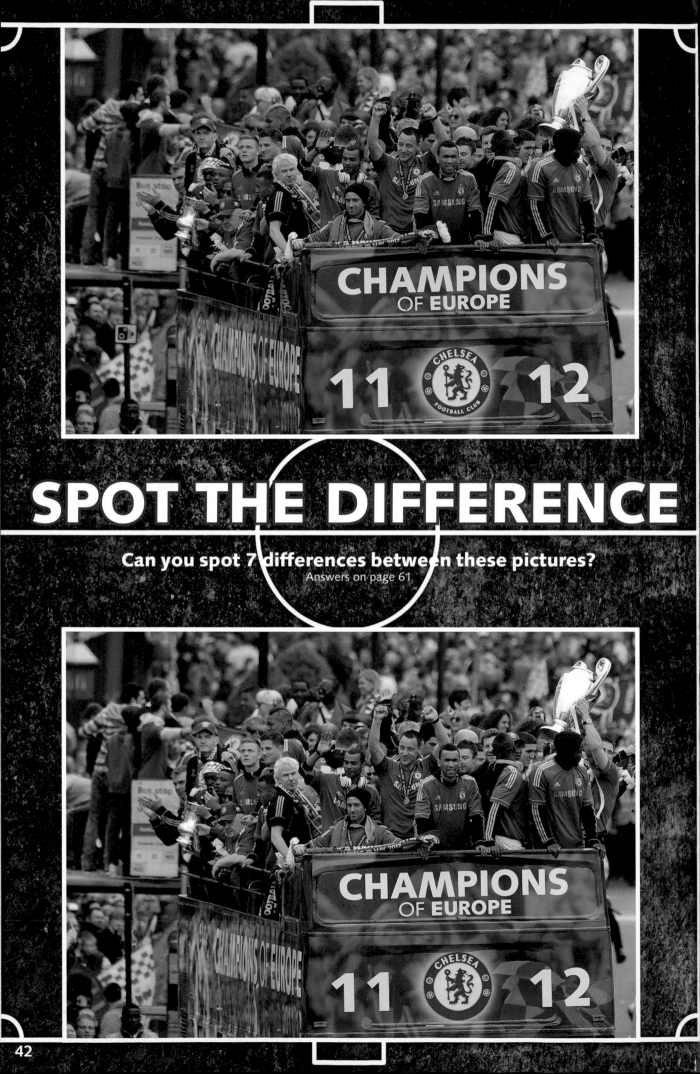

SPOT THE DIFFERENCE

Can you spot 7 differences between these pictures?
Answers on page 61

In honour of Roberto Di Matteo guiding Chelsea to Champions League glory, the 22 names to represent the Blues in our previous European trophy-winning campaign, 1997/98, are hidden below.

They go up, down, backwards and diagonally.

Can you spot them all?

WORDSEARCH

L	G	X	V	N	L	R	A	R	B	T	K	R	T	J
A	T	S	L	I	G	H	I	L	M	N	N	T	K	C
M	E	M	I	Y	A	A	U	S	O	O	D	L	Y	L
B	Y	R	J	P	L	L	L	G	T	Z	E	R	W	A
O	O	L	F	C	R	L	L	W	H	B	R	F	U	R
U	P	F	N	W	O	O	E	I	O	E	N	B	C	K
R	R	I	I	H	Y	N	M	E	B	M	S	O	S	E
D	S	S	C	O	Z	K	U	U	L	X	M	E	E	W
E	E	I	N	R	M	F	D	X	D	L	H	T	R	N
R	N	G	R	A	N	V	I	L	L	E	C	T	T	V
S	B	Y	N	Y	D	Y	E	O	G	E	D	A	E	K
R	C	B	B	A	F	L	O	H	W	W	R	M	P	T
E	J	H	V	B	C	H	A	R	V	E	T	I	B	W
Y	Z	L	Q	A	M	Z	K	Q	F	D	X	D	X	R
M	C	R	M	B	P	T	N	K	X	U	A	S	E	L

Babayaro	Flo	LeSaux	Petrescu
Charvet	Granville	Morris	Poyet
Clarke	Hughes	Myers	Sinclair
DeGoey	Lambourde	Newton	Vialli
DiMatteo	Leboeuf	Nicholls	Wise
Duberry			Zola

Answers on page 61

FA YOUTH CUP

It wasn't just Chelsea's first team who were celebrating FA Cup glory in 2012. It was the Under-18s as well.

After defeating Blackburn Rovers 4-1 on aggregate in a two-legged final, the Blues lifted the FA Youth Cup for the second time in three years – a fantastic achievement.

Coached by Adi Viveash and led on the field by captain Nathaniel Chalobah, this young Chelsea side stuck to their principles of playing the ball out from the back and building attacking moves with accurate passing and effective movement off the ball. Even when things were going against them, they remained true to the methods coached in the Chelsea Academy and it paid off for them in the end.

The youth team also had to show some of the never-say-die spirit made famous by our first team as they recovered from losing positions on several occasions along the way – most incredibly when they came back from 3-0 down to beat Nottingham Forest 4-3, away from home, in the quarter-finals.

After that, last season's winners Manchester United were put to the sword in the semi-finals, before that momentous win over Blackburn sealed the trophy.

The current crop of players may be the Champions of Europe, but the next generation don't look bad either!

THE ROAD TO
FA YOUTH CUP GLORY

Third round
Chelsea 2 Doncaster Rovers 1

Fourth round
Norwich City 0 Chelsea 0
(Chelsea win 4-2 on penalties)

Fifth round
Chelsea 3 West Ham United 3
(Chelsea win 5-4 on penalties)

Quarter-final
Nottingham Forest 3 Chelsea 4

Semi-final (1st leg)
Manchester United 1 Chelsea 2

Semi-final (2nd leg)
Chelsea 1 Manchester United 1
(Chelsea win 3-2 on aggregate)

Final (1st leg)
Chelsea 4 Blackburn Rovers 0

Final (2nd leg)
Blackburn Rovers 1 Chelsea 0
(Chelsea win 4-1 on aggregate)

FA YOUTH CUP WINNERS 2012

Appearances:

Affane	8	
Baker	8	
Blackman	8	
Chalobah	8	
Feruz	8	
Kane	8	
Piazon	8	
Swift	8	
Nditi	7	(1)
Ake	7	
Davey	4	
Kiwomya	1	(6)
Nkumu	1	(4)
A Gordon	1	(2)
Mitchell	1	(1)
Osmanovic	1	
Pappoe	1	
Seremba	0	(2)
Howard	0	(1)
Loftus-Cheek	0	(1)
Nortey	0	(1)

(substitute appearances in brackets)

Goals:

Feruz	6
Piazon	3
Baker	2
Chalobah	2
Affane	1
Kiwomya	1
Swift	1

QUIZ

CHAMPIONS OF EUROPE

1. Which Brazilian player scored the opening goal of Chelsea's UEFA Champions League campaign against Bayer Leverkusen?

2. Can you name the Blues' four goalscorers in the 4-1 victory over Napoli in the second leg of our Round of 16 tie?

3. Which player won Chelsea's Goal of the Season award for the second year in a row after his goal against Barcelona in the semi-finals?

4. How many goals did Didier Drogba score in the UEFA Champions League in 2011/12 to finish as Chelsea's leading scorer?

5. Who was the only Blue to feature in every minute of our UEFA Champions League-winning campaign?

Answers on page 61

BLUE SAID THAT

1 How can you not choose the European champions? Chelsea is one of the biggest clubs in the world; when they are after you, there is no need to even think twice.

2 You are expected to win every game that you play at Chelsea - but that's what you want as a footballer.

3 To win seven FA Cups is amazing. It never gets boring when it comes to lifting that cup - everyone wants to get their hands on it.

4 Now I know what the fans go through every week!

5 If you win the UEFA Champions League regularly, I'm sure it still feels great, but to come so close so many times and then win it feels incredible.

ANAGRAMS

1. A JAM AUNT

2. TIERED MOTORBOAT

Answers on page 61

Birthdays 2012/13 Squad

JANUARY
Ross Turnbull	4/1/85
Eden Hazard	7/1/91
Paulo Ferreira	18/1/79

FEBRUARY
Branislav Ivanovic	22/2/84

MARCH
Fernando Torres	20/3/84
Ramires	24/3/87
Marko Marin	13/3/89

APRIL
John Mikel Obi	22/4/87
David Luiz	22/4/87
Juan Mata	28/4/88

MAY
Petr Cech	20/5/82

JUNE
Florent Malouda	13/6/80
Frank Lampard	20/6/78

JULY

Renew your season ticket!

AUGUST
Ryan Bertrand	5/8/89
Cesar Azpilicueta	28/8/89

SEPTEMBER
Daniel Sturridge	1/9/89
Oscar	9/9/91
Oriol Romeu	24/9/91

OCTOBER
Henrique Hilario	21/10/75

NOVEMBER

DECEMBER
John Terry	7/12/80
Victor Moses	12/12/90
Gary Cahill	19/12/85
Ashley Cole	20/12/80

Tours and more...

As well as getting a guided tour of Stamford Bridge, you can learn all about the Blues' history at the Chelsea Museum.

Stadium tours let you see some of the places not usually open to the public, including the changing rooms and media area, as well as trying out the manager's seat in the pitch-side dugout after walking out the players' tunnel.

All tours finish in the museum, which tells the full 107-year story of Chelsea Football Club and lets you get a closer look at the trophy cabinet, including the FA Cup, Premier League and UEFA Champions League.

Some of the most popular parts of the museum test your football skills with Chelsea heroes from the past and present. You can take on former goalkeeper Peter Bonetti to see if you have the reactions to be a Blues shot stopper with the Beat the Cat Batak game, plus current stars give a video tutorial to help you achieve the perfect finish in the adidas Shooting Gallery.

If that isn't enough, there are also lots of classic shirts donated by Chelsea legends and videos of the Blues' greatest-ever games.

The museum is open seven days a week from 9.30am and closes at 5pm, or at kick-off on Match days. You can book your ticket in advance by calling 0871 984 1955 or going online to www.chelseafc.com/museum.

The Blues' best players of the 2011/12 season were honoured at a glitzy ceremony at Stamford Bridge in May and there were some extremely deserving winners.

At the double

Ramires went home with not one but two trophies after winning the Players' Player of the Year and Goal of the Season. It's not surprising that his team-mates voted for the Brazilian given how much running he does, and how about the "tekkers" he showed for his unbelievable goal against Barcelona in the UEFA Champions League semi-final second leg? Take a bow, Rami!

A Mata of time

Juan Mata was an instant hit at Chelsea, wowing fans with his trickery on the ball, ability to score goals himself, while setting up plenty for his team-mates as well. Little wonder the Spaniard walked away with the main prize on the night, picking up the Player of the Season award as voted for by supporters.

> *It is my first season here so this is even more special for me and I want to thank my team-mates, the staff and all the people who voted for me.*
> Juan Mata

Bright young thing

After winning the FA Youth Cup the night before, Lucas Piazon capped a memorable couple of days by taking home the adidas Young Player of the Year award. The Brazilian attacker is one to watch thanks to his silky Samba skills and eye for goal.

Bobby Tambling

A true legend

While the awards are mainly about honouring current Chelsea players, this year's Special Recognition trophy went to a man who has scored more goals for the club than anybody else. Bobby Tambling wasn't able to attend on the night but his 202 goals for the Blues between 1958 and 1970 make him a deserving winner.

The 2011/12 season saw the Premier League celebrate its 20th birthday! Chelsea is one of just seven clubs to have been in it all that time – and here are some of our best moments...

THE GIFT OF HOD

After a disappointing first season in the Premier League, Chelsea appointed Glenn Hoddle as manager in 1993. He won over the fans by taking the Blues to the FA Cup Final in 1994, and signing world-class players Ruud Gullit and Mark Hughes.

GIANFRANCO ZOLA, LA LA LA!

Blues fans couldn't believe their luck when Gianfranco Zola moved from Parma to Stamford Bridge in November 1996. The Italian showed the kind of skills that most of us could only dream of. He was named Footballer of the Year in his first season at the club after helping us win the FA Cup.

DINING AT EUROPE'S TOP TABLE

Chelsea had been threatening a title challenge for a few years before the 1998/99 season. Tore Andre Flo's double against Blackburn in a 4-3 win was one of the highlights of the campaign in which we finished just four points behind eventual champions, Manchester United. It meant that Chelsea would play in the UEFA Champions League for the first time in our history!

GUS GUNS DOWN UNITED

Man United may have pipped us to the title in 1999, but we had our revenge a few months later in one of the best games ever seen at Stamford Bridge. Gus Poyet scored twice in an unbelievable 5-0 victory, including one goal after just 30 seconds!

" HAVE YOU EVER SEEN CHELSEA WIN THE LEAGUE? "

Yes we have! The arrival of Jose Mourinho as Blues manager in the summer of 2004 helped turn the club into genuine title contenders. A year later we were crowned champions for the second time, exactly 50 years after the first triumph. Frank Lampard scored twice at Bolton, sparking scenes of jubilation as the Blues finished with a record 95 points. And we won the League Cup, too!

THE MAN WITH THE GOLDEN BOOT

Not since the days of Kerry Dixon in the late 1980s and early 1990s had Chelsea had a 20-goal-per-season striker – but that all changed when the club broke its transfer record to sign Jimmy Floyd Hasselbaink from Atletico Madrid. The Dutchman smashed home 23 goals to become the first Blues player to win the Premier League Golden Boot award.

START OF THE ROMAN REVOLUTION

Chelsea needed to avoid defeat against Liverpool in the final game of the 2002/03 season to ensure a place in the following season's UEFA Champions League and, thanks to Jesper Gronkjaer's super-goal, we beat the Reds 2-1! What followed was the most incredible summer in the club's history, as Roman Abramovich bought the Blues and signed some of the world's finest players to turn Chelsea into one of Europe's top clubs.

TWO IN A ROW

To prove our first win was no fluke, the Blues promptly won the championship for a second straight season, beating Manchester United 3-0 at Stamford Bridge to become only the second team to win back-to-back Premier League titles. William Gallas, Joe Cole and Ricardo Carvalho scored the goals, and the title was made all the more special as it came in our centenary year.

BLUES AT THE DOUBLE

It would take something special to top either of our first two Premier League titles – but in 2009/10 the Blues won the title and the FA Cup to do the Double for the first time! What's more, we scored a Premier League record of 103 goals, which included netting seven goals against Sunderland, Aston Villa and Stoke City before we went one better on the final day of the season, beating Wigan Athletic 8-0 to seal the title. A week later, the boys went to Wembley to defeat Portsmouth in the FA Cup Final. "Double, Double, Double – John Terry has won the Double!"

THE INSIDER

The players welcome their new team-mate Gary Cahill to his first training session at Cobham.

Didier Drogba, Michael Essien and Florent Malouda celebrate in the Wembley changing room after winning the FA Cup.

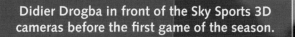

Didier Drogba in front of the Sky Sports 3D cameras before the first game of the season.

Enjoying his first winter in England, Juan Mata starts a snowball fight at training.

Goalkeeper Petr Cech plays the drums on stage for the band Eddie Stoilow in the Czech Republic.

David Luiz poses with a photo of himself at Benfica's stadium before a UEFA Champions League game.

CHELSEA in AMERICA

The Blues travelled to the USA this summer for our sixth pre-season tour Stateside in the space of eight years.

Here are some highlights both on and off the pitch from our previous visits.

The Blues squad enjoyed a spot of sight-seeing around the streets of New York, one of the stop-offs on our 2005 US tour.

Chelsea took on AC Milan for the fifth time on American soil during pre-season this summer. Our last friendly against the Italian side in the USA came in 2009 when we beat them 2-1 at the M&T Bank Stadium in Baltimore.

How many players can you name from this team line-up before our match against Roma at Heinz Field in Pittsburgh in 2004?

David Beckham was a new arrival at LA Galaxy when we beat them 1-0 in a pre-season friendly in 2007 thanks to a John Terry goal.

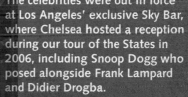

The celebrities were out in force at Los Angeles' exclusive Sky Bar, where Chelsea hosted a reception during our tour of the States in 2006, including Snoop Dogg who posed alongside Frank Lampard and Didier Drogba.

Hollywood stars turned out for our last trip to America in 2009, when Charlize Theron and Will Ferrell showed their support for Chelsea against Inter Milan at the Rose Bowl, California. They proved to be lucky mascots as the Blues won 2-0.

The 2012 trip Stateside might not have featured a trip to Los Angeles, but the Blues did have a couple of Hollywood moments. Comedians Will Ferrell and Zach Galifianakis had the lads in stitches when they visited our hotel in Seattle, while our trip to Philadelphia gave the players a chance to recreate an iconic scene from Rocky!

SPOT THE DIFFERENCE p 42

WORDSEARCH p43

1. David Luiz
2. Didier Drogba, John Terry, Frank Lampard, Branislav Ivanovic
3. Ramires
4. Six
5. Petr Cech

1. Oscar (after completing his move to Chelsea in the summer)
2. Gary Cahill (after joining Chelsea in January from Bolton)
3. Ashley Cole
4. John Terry (after watching the UEFA Champions League Final from the sidelines)
5. Frank Lampard

ANAGRAMS p47

1. A JAM AUNT

2. TIERED MOTORBOAT